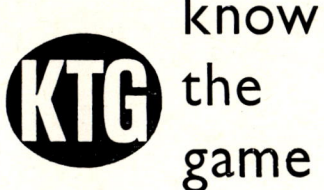

know the game

Lacrosse

Published in collaboration with the
ALL ENGLAND WOMEN'S LACROSSE ASSOCIATION

Contents

Page
- 3 FOREWORD
- 4 HISTORY AND DEVELOPMENT
- 5 THE GROUND
- 5 THE GOAL
- 7 THE STICK
- 7   Care of the stick
- 7 THE BALL
- 8 UNIFORM
- 8 FOOTWEAR
- 9 GOALKEEPER AND EQUIPMENT
- 9 UMPIRES
- 10 POSITIONS ON THE FIELD
- 11 DURATION OF PLAY
- 11 SUBSTITUTES
- 11 THE START OF THE GAME
- 12 THE GRIP
- 13 CRADLING
- 14 TURNING TO RUN IN THE OPPOSITE DIRECTION
- 15 CATCHING
- 16 THE OVERARM PASS
- 18 THE UNDERARM PASS
- 19 PICKING UP A BALL

Page
- 20 MARKING
- 20 GETTING FREE
- 22 DODGING WITH THE BALL PAST AN OPPONENT
- 23 BODY CHECKING
- 24 STICK CHECKING
- 25 OVERARM SHOOTING
- 26 UNDERARM SHOOTING
- 27 GOAL CIRCLE RULES (PLAYERS)
- 27 GOAL CIRCLE RULES (GOALKEEPER)
- 28 GOALKEEPING
- 29 GOAL UMPIRING
- 30 FOULS
- 31   Free position
- 31   The draw
- 32 CENTRE UMPIRING
- 32   Before the game
- 32   During the game; boundaries
- 34 POSITIONAL PLAY
- 36 SIMPLE STRATEGY
- 36   Attack play
- 38   Defence play
- 39 HINTS TO PLAYERS

Foreword

LACROSSE used to be considered a difficult game, suitable only for boarding school conditions, but as a result of changes in methods of coaching it is now being played with enthusiasm and success in secondary schools of all kinds. It is a very fast game because the ball travels through the air by being thrown and caught with the aid of a lacrosse stick. The actions of catching and throwing demand skill, but any girl who reads this book carefully and is prepared to practise can soon become sufficiently proficient to play a lively and energetic game.

The author, Miss Joan Reeson, who played for England for eight seasons, was captain of the English team from 1953 to 1955. She is also a teacher of lacrosse, and the text and illustrations in the book reflect her knowledge and experience in a clear and attractive way. The book is published with the full approval of the All England Women's Lacrosse Association and it is recommended as an invaluable help not only to young players but as a reminder of fundamentals to club players, teachers and coaches.

M. T. Crabbe

President of the All England Women's Lacrosse Association.

Lacrosse

The game of Lacrosse is said to have originated from the Red Indian game of Baggataway, played as a form of tribal celebration. However, a similar game was played in Iceland in the 9th century, so voyaging Norsemen might have introduced it to the Red Indians.

French settlers in Quebec saw the Indians playing the game and called it La Crosse, because the stick used looked like a bishop's crozier. They developed the game and in 1867 it became their national game.

In England men started playing the game in 1876 and ten years later a mixed preparatory school in Manchester took it up; by 1890 a girls' school in Scotland was playing. Originally eight-a-side, by 1899 there were twelve-a-side. The first club for women, 'Southern Ladies,' was started in 1905. Seven years later the Ladies' Lacrosse Association came into existence; this was followed by the Scottish, Welsh and Irish Associations being formed between 1920 and 1930. In 1924, the five territorial associations were founded within the All England Ladies' Lacrosse Association, and both territorial and international matches are played annually. The All England Women's Lacrosse Association, as it is now entitled, together with the territorial and county associations, controls this amateur game, lays down rules, gives advice to all players, and welcomes anyone seeking equipment and coaching.

Here, lacrosse is played from September to March. America has a two months' spring season. The United States Women's Lacrosse Association was founded in 1931. Touring teams play regularly in Great Britain and Ireland, in the U.S.A. and occasionally in Australia.

A team is divided into six attacks and six defences. When in play the ball is kept in the air and rapidly passed from the 'crosses' (the netted part of the stick) of one player to another, goals being scored into a small netted goal. Properly played, with no bodily contact, it is not rough, and an absence of boundaries and no off-side rule make it a very fast game when played by adept players. There are, in fact, very few rules at all.

The players move rapidly up and down the field, often changing positions and making quick attacking movements. Defence players assist by checking and intercepting and beginning the attacking movements.

The main techniques to be learned are the ability to keep the ball in the "crosse" when running or being tackled, and also skill in catching, passing and shooting

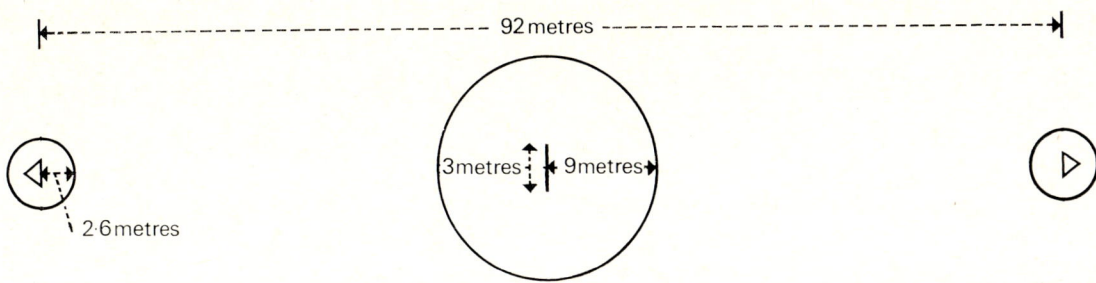

Fig. 1 The ground

The ground

The ground *(Fig. 1)* has no measured boundaries: an area of 110 × 75m is desirable but not essential. A level surface is ideal, but since the ball is kept up in the air, a perfectly smooth surface is not so important as it is with hockey.

The goal

The Goals *(Fig. 2)* are 92m apart, measured from goal line to goal line. The centre circle has a 9m radius with a centre line 3m long. The goal circle is 2.6m radius and each goal consists of two perpendicular posts 1.83m high and 1.83m apart joined at the top by a horizontal cross bar 1.83m from the ground—inside measurement. The white-painted posts should be .05m square and the goal line is drawn from post to post. The netting, of not more than .04m mesh is attached to the posts and crossbar and to a point 1.83m behind the centre of the goal line and must be pegged down firmly. If possible, the netting should be supported from within by a back stay at each end of the cross bar.

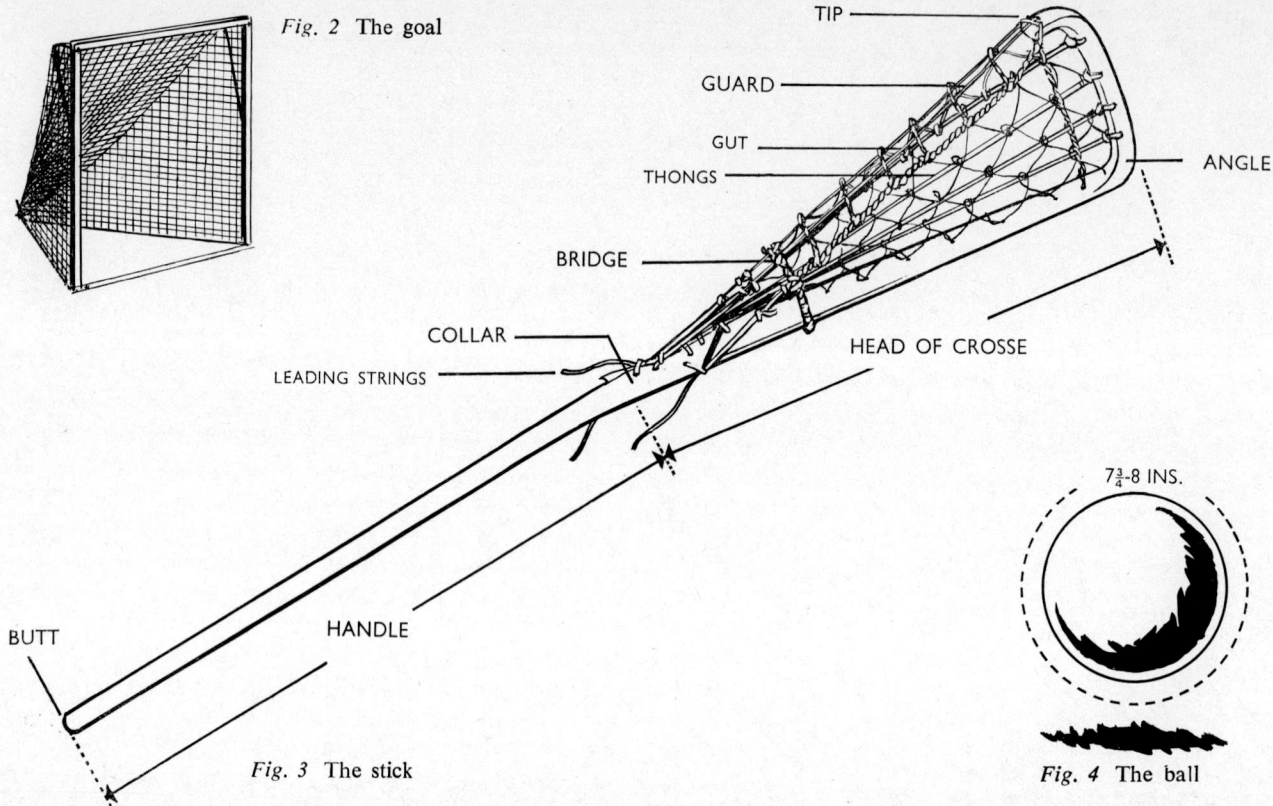

Fig. 2 The goal

Fig. 3 The stick

Fig. 4 The ball

The stick

The stick *(Fig. 3)* is made of hickory and should be bent at slightly more than a right angle before the leading thongs are tightened; the net is made of leather and gut. It may be any length but may not exceed .3m in width and the wood must be on the right hand side of the bridge; left-handed crosses are illegal.

The head of the stick, or "crosse", is made up of the wood from collar to angle forming one wall and the guard, with the leading thongs pulled tight so that the wood beyond the angle lies at 90°, forming the other wall. This is bounded at its lower end by the bridge, necessary to prevent the ball from becoming lodged between the wood and the guard. Between the wood and the guard lie four longitudinal leather thongs interlaced with gut. These thongs are kept at a moderate tension, slack enough to give with the entry of the ball but not to form a pocket for it.

There is no restriction as to the weight of the stick; an average stick will weigh $16\frac{1}{2}$—18 ounces. If the stick is placed on two fingers at the collar it should balance evenly, with a tendency to tip towards the wood. The handle should be approximately the same length as the player's arm.

CARE OF THE STICK

This is very important, not only to preserve the stick but to make the playing of the game easier. The three main leading thongs must always be loosened after play to relieve the strain on the angle. If this is not done the angle becomes affected and the balance of the stick upset, thus making it no longer possible to maintain a firm, upright guard and bridge.

The stick should be dried after use, and kept at a moderate temperature; too much heat dries out both the wood and the gut, and the leather will crack. Neat's Foot Oil is recommended for use on the leather and gut, or white petroleum jelly on the leather thongs alone. The wood should be wiped over occasionally with a cloth soaked in linseed oil.

The ball

The ball *(Fig. 4)*, of black, yellow or white rubber is not less than .20m nor more than .22m in circumference. Weight is between $4\frac{1}{2}$ and 5 ounces. It is therefore about the size and weight of a cricket ball.

Fig. 5 Uniform

Uniform

Most players wear kilts or shorts and shirts with a sweater or cardigan (*Fig. 5*). The uniform chosen should be worn by all members of the team and should be neat, distinctive and comfortable. No player should feel at all restricted in her movements or be unable to stretch easily. The sweater should be the same colour as the shirt to avoid confusion for both players and umpires. Feet are more comfortable if thick socks are worn; these absorb perspiration. Leather gloves are also strongly recommended. Jewellery, metal badges or watches should not be worn; these are not suitable and can be dangerous.

After play, it is sensible to change into fresh clothes to avoid catching cold, preferably washing first if conditions allow.

Footwear

Fig. 6 Footwear

Shoes or boots with rubber soles, preferably having studs and sometimes bars, must be worn, since lacrosse is a game where there are rapid changes of direction.

Goalkeeper and equipment

A goalkeeper should wear sufficient clothes to keep warm but not to hamper movement; trousers or a track suit are quite suitable. She must also have a light pair of leg pads and a body pad *(Fig. 7)*; this usually has leg pieces to protect the thighs. A mask is advisable for goalkeepers who wear glasses.

Umpires

The centre umpire must wear lacrosse boots or shoes and not be hampered by a long skirt or too many layers of outer clothing, and should wear a different colour from that of the players. She needs a whistle, score card, two pencils and a reliable watch (often in representative matches there is a time-keeper at the side of the field). She should also carry a rules book for reference.

The goal umpires, one at each goal, must be mobile and not hampered by too much clothing or players' sweaters; though they must be warm enough, as goal umpiring can be a cold task. Lacrosse boots or shoes should be worn, as a goal umpire must be prepared to move quickly backwards and forwards, and occasionally to the opposite side of the goal. Each goal umpire must have a whistle, score card, pencils, several balls (to provide one quickly if the ball should go far out of play), and a flag with which to signal a goal scored.

Fig. 7 The goalkeeper

Positions on the field

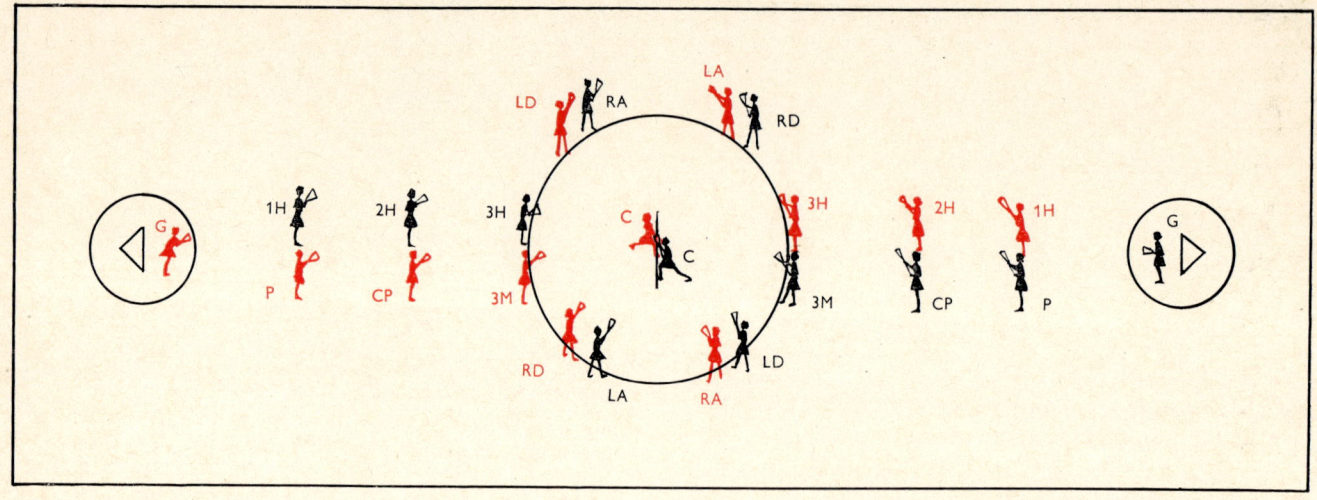

Fig. 8 Positions on the field

There are twelve players in a team, six attacks and six defences *(Fig. 8)*. With the players running at top speed the ball is carried in the crosse or passed through the air from player to player. A goal is scored when the ball is shot into the goal net from in front, propelled by the stick of an attacking player or the stick or person of a defending player.

Defences
G = Goalkeeper
P = Point
CP = Cover Point
3M = Third Man
LD = Left Defence
RD = Right Defence

Attacks
C = Centre
LA = Left Attack
RA = Right Attack
3H = Third Home
2H = Second Home
1H = First Home

Duration of play

The game is played for 50 minutes, unless the captains agree upon a different period of time. At half-time, which may not exceed 10 minutes, the players change ends.

Substitutes

In each team one substitute only is allowed. She may come into the game if a player has an accident or injury which in the umpire's opinion incapacitates her from any further play in the match.

If no substitute is available, or if a further player has to be withdrawn owing to accident or injury, the opposing side must withdraw one of their players for as long as the injured player remains incapacitated, so balancing the two teams.

The start of the game

After the captains have tossed for choice of ends, the players go to their approximate places. They do not need to be placed exactly as in the diagram, but must be at least 9m from the centre line. Play is started by a draw between the two centre players *(Fig. 9)*. A draw is taken at the centre of the field after every goal and after half-time.

At the draw, the players stand with one foot toeing the centre line. The sticks, back to back with the ball between them, are held in the air about hip level, wood to wood, angle to collar, and parallel to the centre line, so that the players' sticks are between the ball and the goals they are defending. On the command "Ready, draw" from the umpire, the opponents immediately draw their sticks up and away from one another: any player may have her right or left hand at the collar, with the other hand at the butt. In this action, the ball is usually thrown into the air, most frequently towards the "Left Attack—Right Defence" position.

Fig. 9
The draw

The grip

Fig. 10a

Fig. 10b

Fig. 10c

Either the right or left hand may be uppermost on the stick. Usually the choice for the top hand is dependent on whether a player throws the ball with her right hand or left hand. With the open part of the crosse facing the player, the V of the thumb and first finger must be placed almost straight on the collar *(Figs. 10a and b)* with all the fingers round the stick. This hand should grip firmly but not quite as strongly as the bottom hand. Here, the hand should be placed at a corresponding angle, with the fingers spread slightly up the stick. The bottom hand, with the elbow bent, holds the stick at waist level and this grip never changes. The top hand, which must not slip down the stick from the collar, keeps the stick vertical, the forearm and elbow being relaxed beside the stick *(Figs. 10b and c)*. This grip does move a little round behind the stick when a pass is made but MUST be corrected again directly the pass is completed. A correct grip is essential.

If the arms relax, with the stick held as above, the head of the stick drops with the wood slightly nearer the ground than the guard.

Cradling

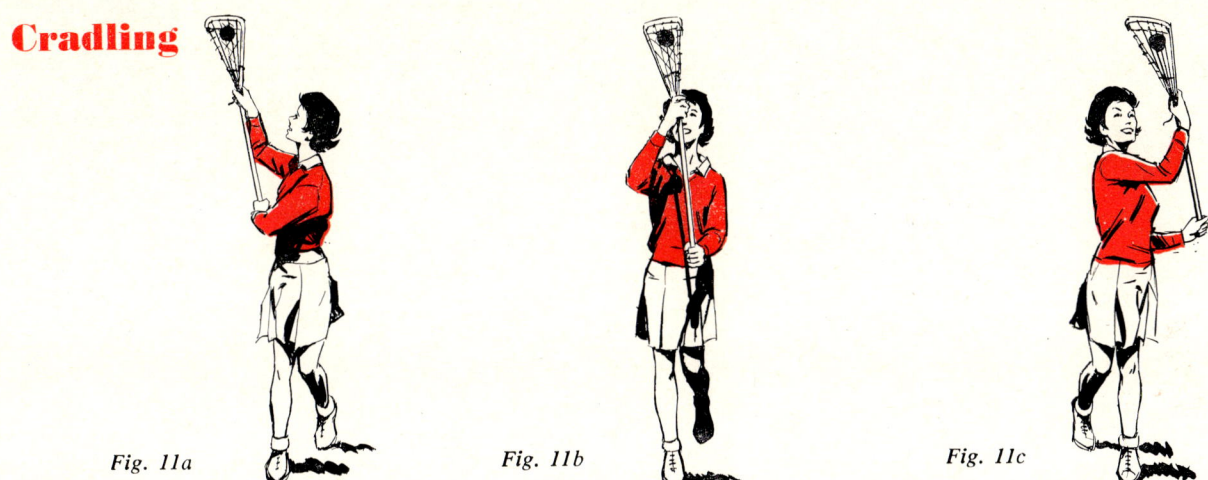

Fig. 11a   Fig. 11b   Fig. 11c

Cradling is the movement of the stick used to keep the ball in the crosse, and is timed to fit in with the running action of the player.

The arms swing together in a rhythmical movement across the body, keeping the stick vertical (for a beginner), and strong flexible movements of both wrists keep the stick encircling the ball *(Fig. 11)*. The elbow and forearm of the top hand remain relaxed and close to the outside of the stick *(Fig. 11a)*, and the shoulders turn slightly with each swing. The bottom hand provides the power and tends to lift a little as the stick is taken to that side; the elbow should be clear of the body *(Fig. 11c)*.

For a beginner, the vertical position of the stick cannot be stressed too much. Begin to cradle while walking, then skipping, breaking into a trot, and running when the rhythm is established. As a player becomes more experienced and runs faster a more oblique cradling position is adopted quite naturally.

Turning to run in the opposite direction

Fig. 12a

Fig. 12b

Fig. 12c

Here a right-handed player is preparing for a turn. She will turn right about. This is important to master at an early stage in learning the game, and is merely a development of cradling from one side to the other to enable a player to elude her opponent.

With one foot in front of the other, the player swings her stick round her whole body, whilst she pushes strongly off her front foot, the knee of that leg being well bent *(Figs. 12a and b)*. Having turned, she continues to cradle in front of her and to run in the opposite direction without a pause *(Fig. 12c)*. The movement is initiated by the push from the front foot combined with the shoulder turn. The feet are both kept on the ground in the pivot turn which "unwinds" the player's legs.

Catching

Fig. 13   *Fig. 14*   *Fig. 15*   *Fig. 16*

Catching is cradling! The player moves her arms in the cradling action to get the stick to the place where the ball is wanted, or is being sent, making sure, by using both wrists, that the face of the crosse is turned fully towards the ball. The ball should be watched into the widest part of the crosse and, as it touches, the arms and wrists swing with "give" and relaxation round the ball, and cradling is continued. To be safe, the catch should always be made so that the stick moves inwards towards the body. Players must be able to catch balls coming at all heights and in any direction *(Figs. 13, 14 and 15). Remember* to relax more for a ball travelling very fast. Try to increase speed as the ball is caught, not to slow down or stop running.

A ball coming towards a player on or just off the ground is similar to a low catch, but to get the stick upside down requires daring *(Fig. 16)*. Good footwork is essential to get the right foot (for a right-handed player) beside the ball as it is caught, with a give backwards, in the crosse, yet with the feet continuing to run forward.

15

The overarm pass

The action of this pass follows naturally on to cradling:

(a) The stick is swung to the left (for a right-handed player) as though the player is going to run in the opposite direction *(Fig. 17a)* (see also Page 14).

(b) The stick swings to the right with the bottom hand coming to that side as the right shoulder is taken back, and the grip of the top hand slides slightly behind the stick *(Fig. 17b)*.

(c) The right elbow bends fully and the left hand is lifted a little while pointing to where the stick is to move *(Fig. 17c)*.

(d) A strong pull of the lower hand upwards into the armpit, together with the stretch upwards and forwards of the right arm pointing the stick to where the ball is going, completes the pass *(Fig. 17d)*. The ball should run up the stick close to the wood for a right-handed player, and near the guard for a left-handed player. The inter-timing of the action of both arms together is very important, and the rhythm of the player's run must not be broken as the pass is made.

Fig. 17a.

Fig. 17b

Fig. 17c

Fig. 17d

(e) During this pass it is useful to pretend that the player is twice her height and point to that spot, then the ball will arrive at a perfect height easy for a player to catch without breaking the rhythm of her cradling *(Fig. 18).* This pass is known as the shoulder pass. Overarm passes can be done in similar ways at different levels down to the horizontal plane where the pass is called the sling or lever pass.

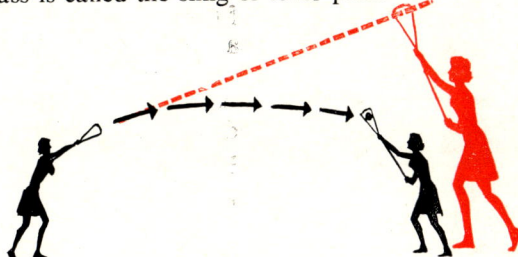

Fig. 18

To pass to the left (for a right-handed player), less shoulder turn is needed, but to pass to the right a very big turn of the shoulders is required. Passes can be direct or hanging, depending on a quick strong pull in of the lower hand or an upward swinging movement of the stick.

As soon as the pass is completed the player resumes her cradling, remembering to correct the "V" grip of her top hand *(see Page 12, Fig 10).*

The underarm pass

This should be learned only after every variation of the overarm pass has been mastered. The overarm pass is more accurate and is checked less easily.

In the underarm pass, a right-handed player *(Fig. 19a)* turns the upper part of the body further to the left than in the overarm pass, cradling the stick to that side *(Fig. 19b)*, then the head of the stick is dropped towards the ground in a semi-circular motion *(Fig. 19c)*. Without pause the stick is swung forward close past the knees, finishing ahead of the body with the wood turned slightly towards the ground, the ball rolling the length of the wood before leaving the crosse *(Fig. 19d)*.

The movement of the top hand in relation to these positions is shown in *Fig. 19e*.

A left-handed player also turns the wood to the ground so that in this case the face of the crosse turns away from her.

The height of the pass is controlled by the amount of lift of the stick at the end of the movement, the length by the push from the lower arm, and the direction by the amount of shoulder turn into the follow-through. The underarm shot is the same action, but the head of the stick is kept low in the follow-through (see Page 26, Fig. 28d).

Figs. 19a, b, c, d

Fig. 19e

MOVEMENT OF TOP HAND

Picking up a ball

For a stationary ball the head should be well over the ball, and the stick, foot and ball are as close together as possible *(Fig. 20)*. To get into this position a player should:

(a) Begin to bend her knees at least four steps away from the ball.
(b) Cradle the stick to the side of her lower hand with the opposite shoulder well forward.
(c) Push the stick straight forward along the ground under the ball, having her foot close beside the ball, and letting the arms go forward.
(d) Continue this forward movement with stick parallel to the body, cradling gradually higher and higher from the ground (rather like going upstairs) until a vertical position is regained. More experienced players require only one cradling movement to reach the vertical.

For a ball rolling away, the action is exactly as for a stationary ball except:

(a) The player must be moving faster than the ball.
(b) The push with the lower hand is stronger to get the ball into the crosse.
(c) The player must increase speed as the pick-up is made.

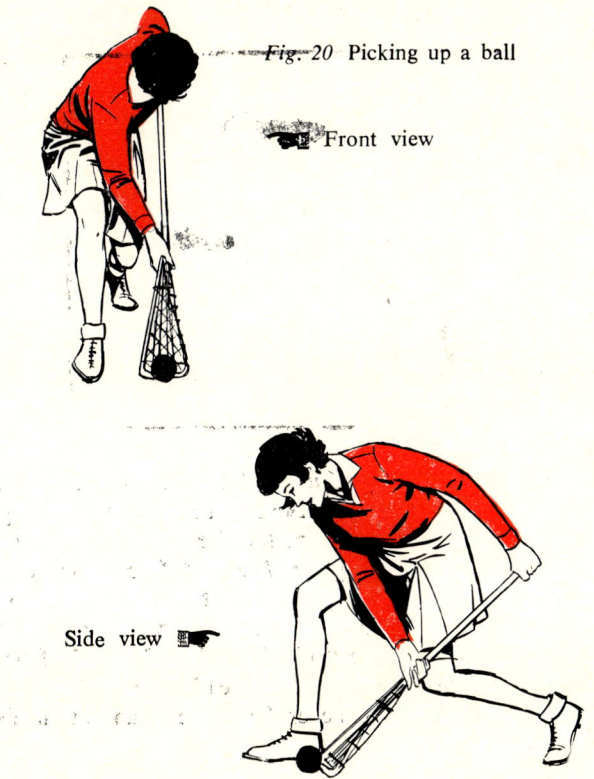

Fig. 20 Picking up a ball

Front view

Side view

Marking

Getting free

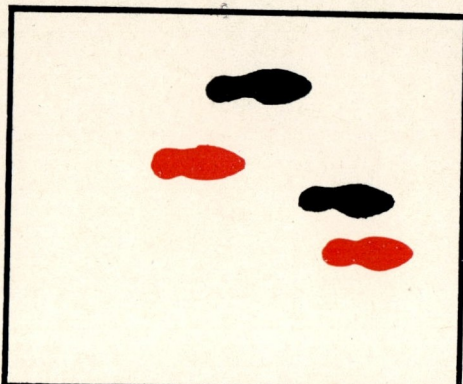

Fig. 21

Figs. 22a, b, c, d

Marking is very important in lacrosse as the whole strategy is dependent on close man-to-man marking. The ideal position is with one foot behind her opponent and the other foot alongside *(Fig. 21)*. She is ready to come forward to intercept a pass if she is quick and certain of success. She can move back on to the path of her opponent, goal side, to body and stick check if her opponent is able to get the ball. Ideally she is always as close, but she should never be more than an arm's length away.

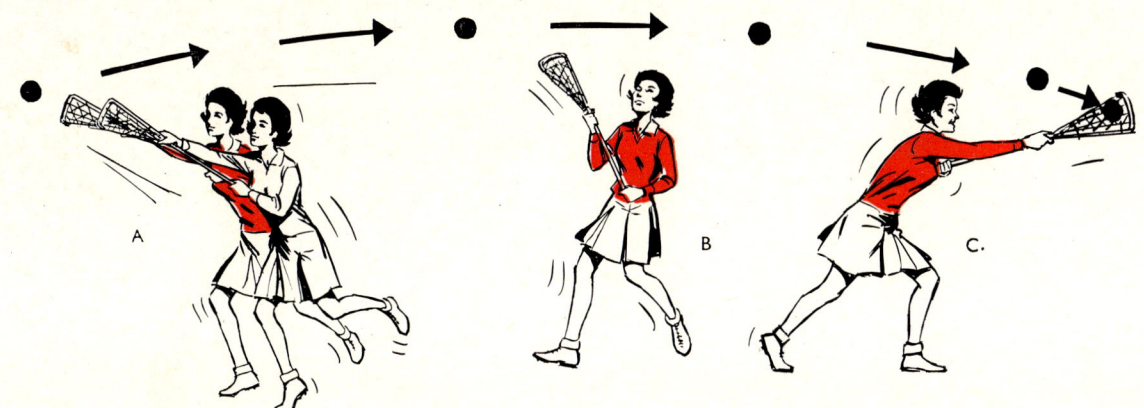

Figs. 23a, b, c

One way of getting free is shown in *Fig. 22*.

(a) Running this way she is just free enough to catch an accurate pass into the space ahead of her *(Fig. 22a)*.

(b) She changed direction quickly as she did not receive the pass, and her stick is already leading her movement *(Fig. 22b)*.

(c) By her sudden change of direction she has a definite lead over her opponent and is watching the player with the ball *(Fig. 22c)*.

(d) Although closely marked she is free again to receive a pass *(Fig. 22d)*.

Other ways of getting free are:

(a) To run a few steps in the opposite direction or merely change weight definitely on to the back foot and then sprint forward to receive a short direct pass.

(b) To take a few steps forward *(Fig. 23a)*, turn quickly and run diagonally away from your opponent to receive a hanging pass *(Figs. 23b and c)*. This is not as effective since it is more easily intercepted.

(c) To sprint suddenly from a gentle walk or trot into a space. This should be used only when a player really is much faster than her opponent.

Dodging with the ball past an opponent

Fig. 24a

Fig. 24b

To do this successfully, the player must change her speed just before she can be tackled. She begins her dodge by swinging her stick to the side away from her opponent with a big shoulder turn *(Fig. 24a)*, continuing to cradle smoothly on that side of her and running obliquely forward with quick small steps. Her stick should be kept close, and not left behind her. If her opponent is still tackling her too much for freedom of play *(Fig. 24b)*, she must swing her stick quickly and with a big shoulder turn to the opposite side, moving her feet very quickly to this diagonal. She must increase her speed in her dodge, but may possibly not succeed until she has made several dodges.

Body checking

Fig. 25a

Fig. 25b

If an interception has not been possible, and the opponent has the ball, the defending player places herself between that opponent and her objective, the goal [this is known as "goal side" *(Fig. 25a)*], and she must body check her opponent, moving without touching her to make her pass or force her off her direct path to goal *(Fig. 25b)*. Quick neat footwork, small steps and even balance are essential. A defence's body and stick movements should try to copy exactly those of her opponent, changing direction with her but always facing her.

Stick checking

Fig. 26a Fig. 26b Fig. 26c

Whilst moving backwards and body checking, the defending player reaches forward with her stick held vertically and fairly high and makes small tapping movements to dislodge the ball; "nibbling" away continuously, downwards, sideways, or, if upwards, it must be with a very small controlled movement.

To body check an approaching attack coming fast, a defending player should "shadow" her opponent's stick movements and begin to move backwards before the attack reaches her. Then she can move with the attack as she makes her dodge *(Fig. 26a)*. If she fails, she should chase her opponent and stick check from behind *(Fig. 26b)*, but she must make sure that she keeps her hands at the collar and butt of her stick *(Fig. 26c)*.

Overarm shooting

Figs. 27a, b, c, d Overarm shooting

This is a similar action to the overarm pass, but the stick is lifted high *(Fig. 27a)*, close to the head, until the top arm is nearly straight *(similar to the position in Fig. 27c)*. Without pause, there should be a quick bend of the top elbow *(Fig. 27b)* followed by a strong flick with both wrists, pulling the bottom hand close into the opposite armpit as the top arm swings forwards *(Fig. 27c)* and downwards to point the angle of the stick where the ball should go *(Fig. 27d)*.

Shots at ankle height placed to the corners of the goal are most difficult to save; though, on a very hard or soft, slippery pitch, a shot up to two feet short of the goalkeeper which bounces to an uncertain height is extremely tricky for a goalkeeper to judge. Shots at waist height, particularly on the goalkeeper's non-stick side, are also effective.

An attack should not attempt to shoot high until she has become very skilled. Then her stick must be high and with a light, very wristy movement, she shoots softly into a top corner.

Underarm shooting

Figs. 28a b, c, d Underarm shooting

This is exactly similar to an underarm pass (see Page 18), but the preparatory turn of the shoulders away from goal should be exaggerated *(Fig. 28b),* with a strong turn forward of the shoulders as the stick swings past the body *(Fig. 28c)* into the follow-through *(Fig. 28d)* and the head of the stick is kept low.

Practise shooting from every angle, including coming round from behind the goal. All attacks should be able to catch on the reverse side, lift their sticks and shoot accurately with no extra cradling movement: this is known as "Catch-lift-shoot".

Goal circle rules (players)

A goal is scored by the whole ball passing over the goal line and under the crossbar from in front, propelled by the stick of an attacking player, or by the stick or person of a defending player.

When shooting or passing, a player may not have any part of her body or stick over the crease either during or after a shot or pass *(Fig. 29)*. Uncontrolled, dangerous shots are penalised. After a shot she may not run into or through the crease nor may she reach forward with her stick over the crease when tackling the goalkeeper with the ball. However, any player may run through or across the goal to field a wide ball.

For any infringement of these rules, the goalkeeper is given a "free position" (see Page 31).

Goal circle rules (goalkeeper)

The goalkeeper, whilst within the crease, may stop the ball with her hand or body as well as her stick. If it is caught with her hand she may put the ball in her crosse.

If the goalkeeper leaves the goal circle for any reason, any one player who goes into the goal circle to deputise for her automatically has the goalkeeper's privileges.

If the ball becomes lodged in the goalkeeper's pads whilst within the circle she may remove the ball and place it in her crosse.

When she has the ball within the crease she must clear at once. She must be careful not to take her stick with the ball back over the goal line.

She is allowed to draw the ball back into the crease provided that both feet are within the crease. When outside the crease with the ball (black arrow) she may not step back into the crease (red arrow) nor run across until she has passed the ball *(Fig. 30)*.

Any defence player may run into the goal circle to field a ball there, whilst the goalkeeper is also within the crease.

For any infringement of these rules see page 31.

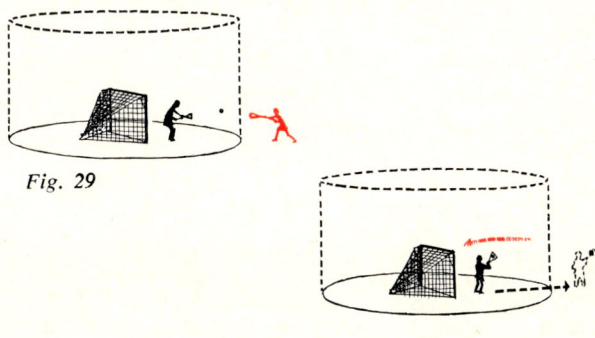

Fig. 29

Fig. 30

Goalkeeping

The goalkeeper must appear cool, calm and collected to give confidence to her team, and she should feel that she is the first attack. She should have a good eye and quick reaction, great power of concentration, be quick on her feet and have excellent stickwork to get both her stick and body behind every shot at goal. Ideally, she should catch every ball shot so that no ball could rebound off her stick or pads out of the circle to give her opponents another opportunity to shoot. If the ball is in her stick she can begin her own team's attack at once, either with a short pass or a long accurate clear of up to 50 yards. Whenever she could be first on to a loose ball, or to collect a wide pass she should run out of goal, so control of a good dodge is also essential for the moment when she is tackled out of the goal circle.

Stand relaxed with feet close together, weight on balls of feet. Head of stick should be low and held slightly in front of body. A right-handed player should stand slightly to the left centre of goal, leaving a little more to cover on the stick side of the body.

Watch the ball, not only the player and her eyes.

Move with quick side steps on the arc of a circle in order to narrow the angle *(Fig. 31a)*, and not along the goal line *(Fig. 31b)*, continually repositioning as the game approaches, to cover the line of any shot made from any angle. When the ball is coming down the wing, feel for the post with hand or stick, trying wherever possible to move so close that no shot can go between post and body—shots made then could be successful only from the other side or high

Move forward to the ball if possible and clear before the opposing team can get back to mark or intercept.

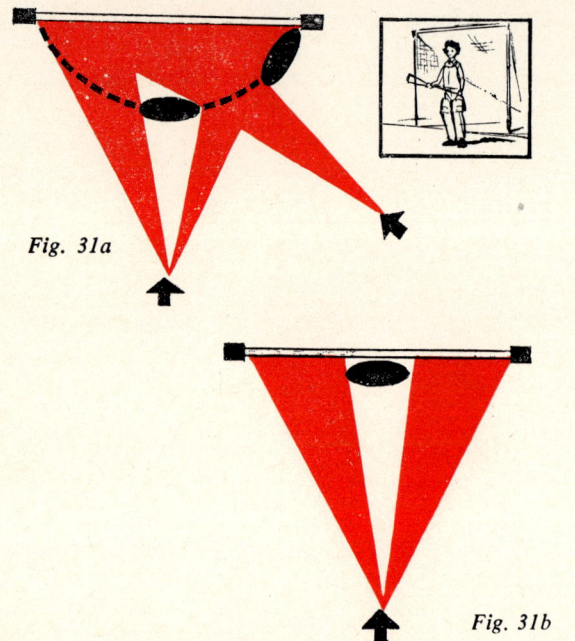

Fig. 31a

Fig. 31b

Goal umpiring

For rules of the goal circle see page 27.
The duties of the goal umpire are as follows:

(a) She must remain at the same goal throughout the match and be responsible for the rules concerning the crease.

(b) Before the match she should check that the netting is attached firmly to the goalpost and is securely pegged down at the back. No balls should be left in the goal, nor sweaters behind the goal.

(c) When a goal is scored she signals by raising her flag until the centre umpire blows the whistle.

(d) She must keep an accurate record of the order in which goals are scored by each player at her goal.

(e) If there is any infringement of the rules, she blows her whistle at once to stop the game. The centre umpire then awards the penalty.

(f) She must have spare balls ready so that she can give one to a player if the game is stopped because the ball goes far out of play.

The goal umpire must be ready to move quickly forwards or backwards, and occasionally to the opposite side of the goal, since she must always be at right angles to the line of approach to goal of the player with the ball, and when the goalkeeper is being tackled *(Fig 32).*

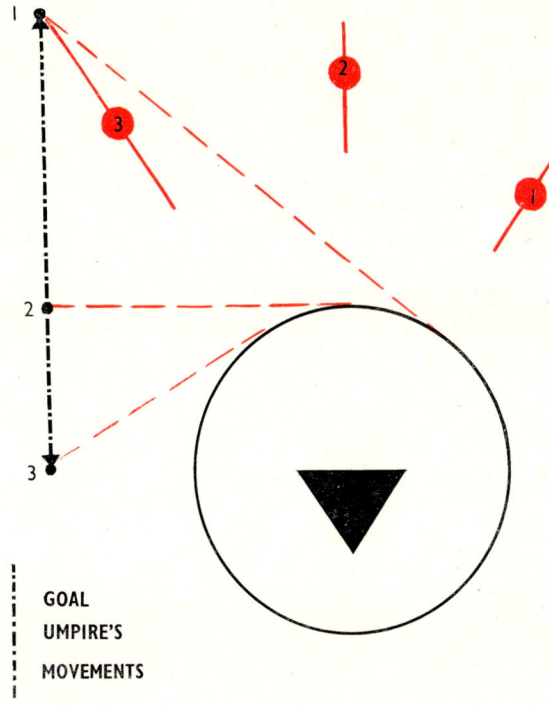

Fig. 32

Fouls

Figs. 33a, b, c, d Fouls

A player may not:

(a) Roughly check an opponent's stick. This can happen with too hard a tackle or where the stick is held down; or by a player slipping her top hand when she has been beaten, to try to check again *(Fig. 33a).*

(b) Deliberately check an opponent's stick when she is trying to get possession of the ball *(Figs 33b and c).*

(c) Detain an opponent by pressing against her body or stick with the arm or stick. Body checking is allowed where the players are not touching (see page 23, *Fig. 25*).

(d) Charge or shoulder an opponent, nor push with the hand *(Fig. 33d).*

(e) Push her opponent off a ground ball, nor guard a ground ball with her foot or crosse. This does not prohibit stopping a rolling ball.

(f) Guard her crosse with her arm.

(g) Trip an opponent.

(h) Touch the ball with her hand except for the goalkeeper (see page 27).

(i) Propel the ball with her foot, leg or body to her own team's advantage.

(j) Throw her stick, nor, unless she has possession of her stick, impede an opponent in any way.

The umpire, on seeing a foul, blows her whistle and calls "Stand": no player may move after this. The penalty for a foul is a "free position", except where two players foul simultaneously, and then a draw is taken.

FREE POSITION

The umpire shows the player taking the free position where to stand, and all the other players must be 5 metres away. The offending player is placed by the umpire according to the severity of the foul. The player awarded the free position takes the ball in her crosse and when the umpire calls "Play" she may run, pass or shoot and the play proceeds.

A free position is never taken within 10 metres of the goal line by an attacking player, the position in front of the goal being decided by the umpire, again according to the severity of the foul. If the foul prevented an almost certain goal, the umpire may order one or more players, including the goalkeeper, from between such a free position and the goal.

THE THROW

The throw is taken where the foul occurred, except that it must be 10 metres from the goal and from the decided boundary. All other players must be 5 metres away (*Fig. 34*).

The two players shall stand at least one metre apart with the defending player good side. The umpire shall stand with her back to the centre of the game between 5 and 10 metres from the two players. On the word 'play' the umpire shall throw the ball with a short, high throw so that the players take it as they move in towards the game (*Fig. 35*).

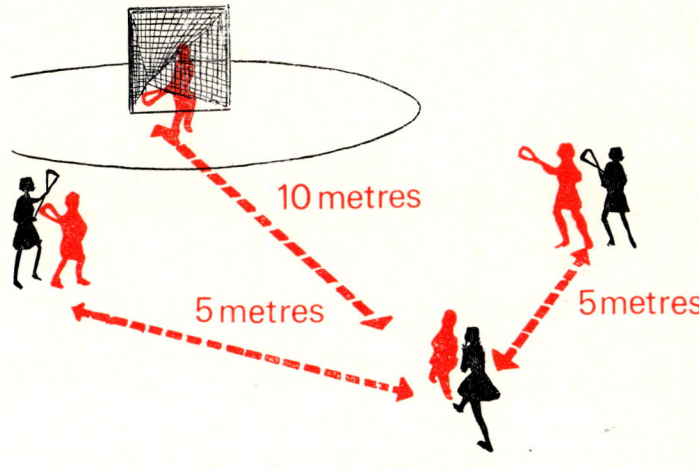

Fig. 34   Figure shows the throw

Centre umpiring

BEFORE THE GAME

The umpire should meet the goal umpires to see that the goal posts are upright and firm, that the goal nets are attached firmly and pegged down to the ground, the markings on the field correct, and that the ball is suitable. She will also check their duties with them.

She will then see that the captains toss for choice of ends and with them will decide on the boundaries and agree on the playing time.

In an important representative match she may have a timekeeper at the side of the field.

DURING THE GAME

The centre umpire must be firm and decisive at all times.

At the centre draw she checks that players are in their relative positions, makes sure sticks are correctly placed for the draw, moves away from the probable direction of the ball, and calls "Ready, draw".

Then she strives to keep well up with the ball and the play, roughly on a line through the side of the centre circle from goal to goal, but not in the players' way. She must enforce the rules, whistling quickly if a foul should occur and awarding penalties without delay.

She also keeps time and records the score.

The goal umpire raises her flag if a goal is scored, and the centre umpire blows her whistle. If there is any infringement of the rules relating to the crease, the goal umpire blows her whistle to stop the game and the centre umpire then awards the penalty.

In the case of an accident or stoppage for any other reason (such as a dog going off with the ball) the umpire stops the game, notes the time and adds it to the half in which the stoppage occurs. The game is re-started with a throw unless the accident has been caused by rough play, when a free position is given (see Page 11 re substitutes). If the game is stopped for an accident quite unrelated to the position of the ball when the whistle is blown the game is re-started merely by the ball being given to the player who was in possession or nearest to it at the time play was stopped.

When the ball goes beyond the decided boundaries, the umpire blows her whistle and calls "Stand". No player may move after this. The nearest player then takes the ball and on the word "Play" the game proceeds: on this occasion another player may be within 5 metres as this is not a free position. If two players are equally near the ball, a throw is taken.

The umpire moves the player or players if it should be necessary so that they are at least 10 metres from the goal line.

A throw is taken if the ball should become lodged in the clothing of a player. If the ball becomes lodged in the crosse, the crosse must be struck on the ground, and if the ball is not dislodged immediately, the game is stopped and a throw taken where the player caught the ball.

If the ball goes into goal off a non-player a throw is taken 10 metres from the goal, the umpire deciding on the position.

As in other ball games the umpire should "hold" her whistle, that is, refrain from putting any rule into effect if by enforcing it she would penalise the non-offending team, but she should indicate she has seen the foul by saying 'play on'.

The umpire's decision is always final.

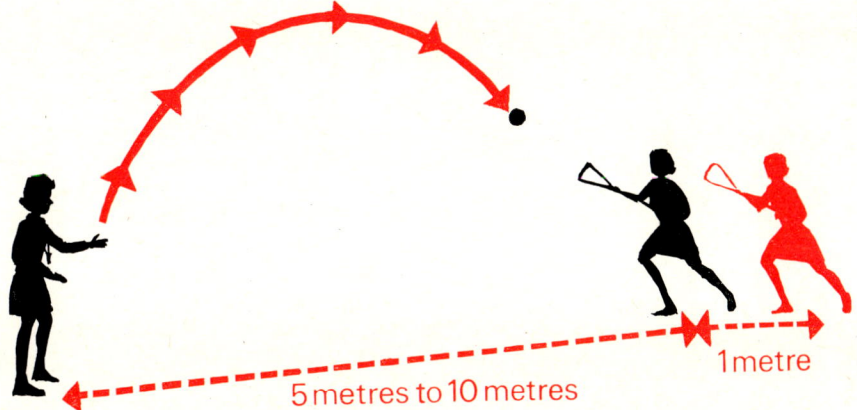

Fig. 35 Players stand five to ten metres from the umpire and side by side about a metre apart

Positional play

The Goalkeeper

should have very good stickwork and quick reactions, she should try to anticipate from which direction the ball is coming by watching the ball and the player, and getting her body behind it. She must aim to catch any shot rather than stop the ball from going into goal. She should field wide balls out of goal whenever possible, and make constructive clears or passes to begin the attack.

Point

should mark First Home closely and tackle another player only in dire emergency. She should go into goal when the goalkeeper is out of the circle.

Cover Point

is known as the pivot of the defence; she must have good, close stickwork and be quick to think and to move. She must mark Second Home closely, yet be quick enough to get on to the path of any free player to body and stick check before she can shoot. She must aim to deflect a shot if she cannot prevent it. Interception is valuable.

Third Man

should mark Third Home closely, be adept at intercepting, and tackle Centre only if she comes on to her path when Third Home is alongside or further away from goal. She should begin the attack whenever possible.

Left and Right Wing Defences

should mark Right Attack and Left Attack closely when the ball is on their side of the field. They should cover in the middle of the field ready to mark Second Home if Cover Point goes to tackle another player, or First Home, if Point goes off in an emergency; and initiate attacking movements. Right Defence must be particularly ready to catch the ball from a centre draw.

Centre

should learn to control the draw. She should mark the opposing Centre closely, and be the link between defences and attacks, spreading the game and initiating many attacking movements.

Left and Right Wing Attacks

should keep well out on the wing. The ball should be fetched from Third Man level (far edge of circle) and speed used to begin and keep up with the attack. They should be the arrowhead of the attack in learning to shoot accurately to the far corner of the goal from a wide angle, and from as far away as Second Home level, and always be ready to tackle, as well as to intercept a clear. Left Attack hopes to get the ball from a centre draw.

Third Home

should initiate most of the homes' movements, learn to dodge well, use acceleration and move from the centre line to the Second Home level. When the opening is made, she should cut straight to goal to shoot.

Second Home

should balance the homes' positioning, be able to accelerate quickly in dodging to get free, and make the most of the Cover Point-Wing Defence interchange so that the Wing Defence cannot mark her when Cover Point has to leave to tackle another player. She must be very quick and accurate in a wide variety of shots.

First Home

should make moves to as far away as Third Home level, to the goal, and round it. She must be very quick in dodging and changing direction, and be able to catch and-shoot without extra cradling movements. (All Homes should be able to do this and should have control of a wide variety of shots.) She should field all wild shots at goal, be prepared to play behind the goal, and always be quick to tackle the goalkeeper when she has the ball.

Simple strategy

ATTACK PLAY

From the draw, attacks should always be on the move, ready to accelerate in any direction. If an attack makes her move but does not have the ball passed to her at once, she must make a second dodge in another direction to reposition and help again; this avoids crowding and enables players to make their moves in conjunction with each other. Exchanging positions, i.e. interchanging, should be encouraged when team players play together regularly and know each other's movements.

In lacrosse, either you make a space for yourself to move into or a space for someone else. About 5 yards in any direction is enough for a home when dodging to get free. All attacks must have plenty of ideas and vary their dodges so that they can outwit a close-marking defence, yet they must be quick to tackle back and do their share of defending when their team loses the ball.

When the ball is near goal, the wing attacks should be around Second Home level and make their moves to converge on the goal posts like an arrowhead *(Fig. 36)*.

Open spacing, no crowding of players, and swinging the ball quickly to the opposite side of the field make for a good game and make it hardest for the defences *(Fig. 37a)*. *(Fig. 37b)* shows an alternative final pass, termed a triangular pass.

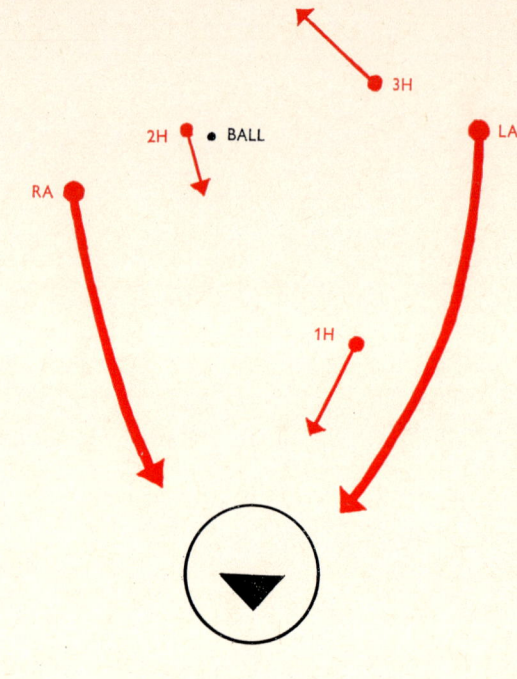

Fig. 36

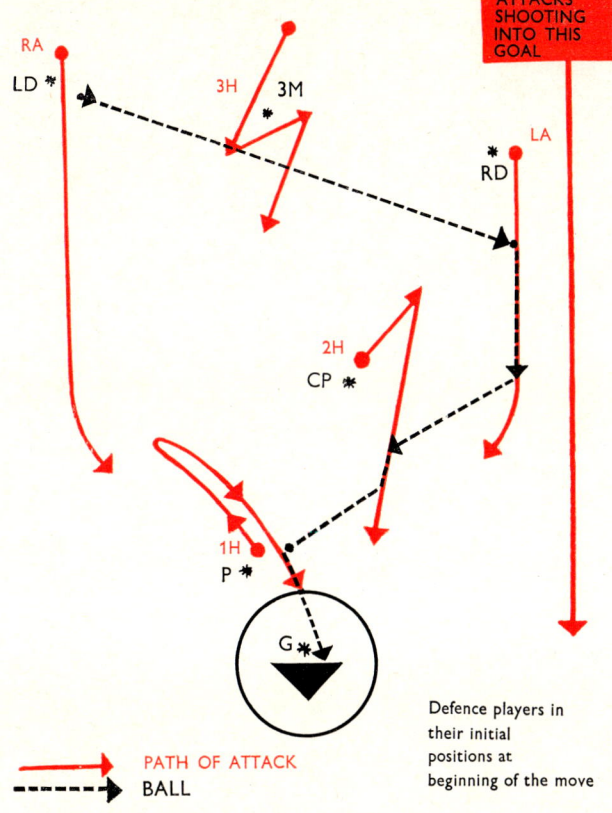

Defence players in their initial positions at beginning of the move

PATH OF ATTACK
BALL

Fig. 37a

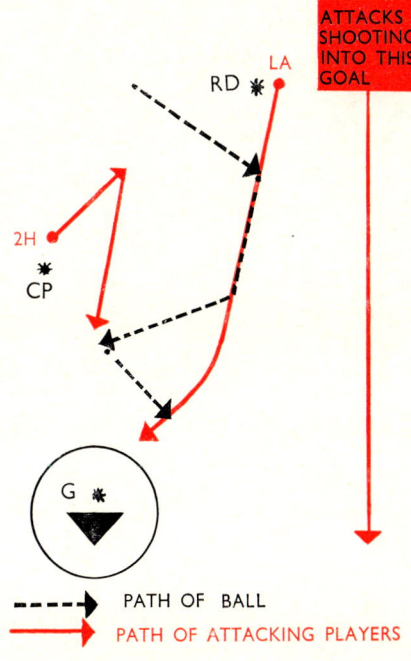

PATH OF BALL
PATH OF ATTACKING PLAYERS

Fig. 37b

DEFENCE PLAY

The object of defence play is not only to prevent a goal being scored but to gain possession of the ball.

A defence should mark her opponent on the goal side, keeping not more than an arm's length distance at any time. She will then be able to body check and, if she is quick-footed, keep on the path of an attack as she runs towards goal even if the player tries to dodge past her. She must be ready to check an opponent's stick continually and in any direction with light, jabbing movements of her stick. She should intercept only when she thinks she is certain of success.

She must be able to clear quickly and accurately, enjoy beginning the attack, and be very quick to reposition on the goal side of a member of the opposing team if she should be outwitted.

Cover Point, or Point in emergency, must be prepared to tackle any free player *(Fig. 38)*, therefore the Wing Defences must be ready to mark Second or First Home from the goal side when the ball is not on their side of the field.

A defence aims to get the ball, but, if she does not succeed at first, she must force her opponent to pass or at any rate be deflected off her straight path to goal until she does succeed and can begin the attack.

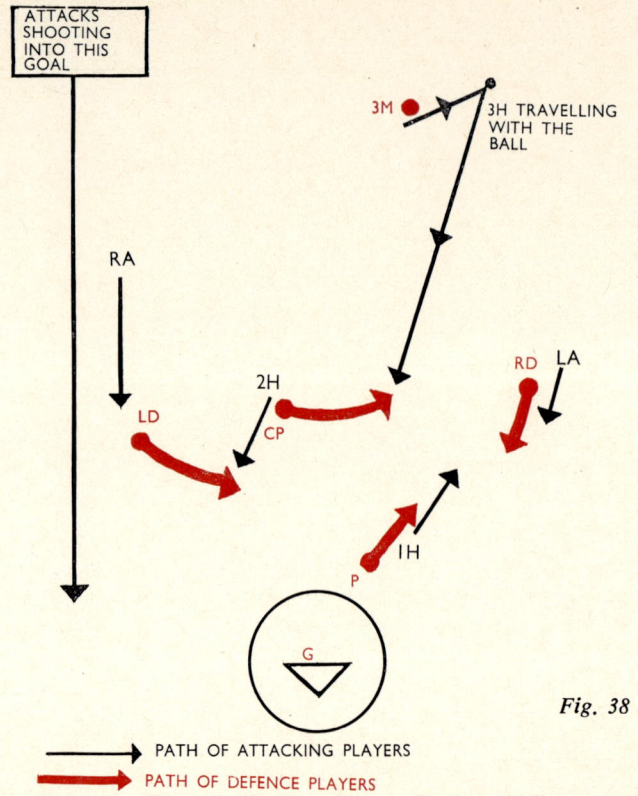

Fig. 38

Hints to players

1. Make sure your stick is kept in good condition, clean, oiled and greased regulary.
2. At the beginning of the season, practise as much as possible to loosen yourself up.
3. Practise overarm passes at different levels and control a swinging underarm pass; all passes must be accurate. Try to vary your passes in a game.
4. Since a ball travels faster than you can run, pass quickly and at once reposition yourself to help again.
5. Never slow down to pass, pick-up or catch. Keep moving.
6. Send the ball into the space ahead of a player, then she can catch it without losing speed. Two players can practise this together.
7. Disguise your intention until you pass, or your opponent can have too good a chance to intercept the ball.
8. Pass immediately the ball is asked for.
9. Quick, short passes are best amongst the attacks.
10. Always be punctual and, above all, enjoy the game of lacrosse as a member of a team.

ALL ENGLAND WOMEN'S LACROSSE ASSOCIATION

Facilities available to lacrosse players:—

1. Membership of the A.E.W.L.A. as an individual, or through affiliation in a club, college or school.
2. Inter club-and-college, or inter-school tournaments.
3. Opportunity for selection in international, territorial, county, and junior county teams (in some areas).
4. Coaching courses for players and umpires.
5. Coaches can be provided.
6. (a) Sets of loan equipment are available for three months to any school, club or college wishing to play lacrosse.
   (b) Equipment may be hired for a further period until groups purchase their own equipment.

ALL ENGLAND WOMEN'S LACROSSE ASSOCIATION—*Publications*

Lacrosse—Playing and Coaching, by Margaret Boyd, O.B.E., £1.05, postage 8p.)

Do's and Dont's, by International Players (12½p Postage 3½p)

Lacrosse, Notes on Umpiring, by Cecily M. Read, Revised 1959 by I. Nowell-Smith (10p, postage 3p)

Know the Game—Lacrosse, by Educational Productions Ltd. in co-operation with Miss J. Reeson, (25p, postage 4p)

Rules Books (8p, postage 3p)

Seven-a-Side Rule Books (5p, postage 3p)

Wall Charts (20p each, postage 5p)

Play Lacrosse the Easy Way, by B. J. Lewis (25p, postage 4p)

Pick a Practice, by B. J. Lewis, (25p, postage 3p)

Umpires Score Cards (1 for 3p, 10 for 25p, plus postage)

Team Lists (1 for 4p, 10 for 30p, plus postage)

Posters (1p, plus postage)

NOTE These prices apply when going to print.

All obtainable from Mrs J. A. Herton, 56 Copthorne Road, Leatherhead, Surrey (Leatherhead 72689)

'*Lacrosse*', official Magazine of the A.E.W.L.A. 75p per season, post free in U.K. only obtainable from: Organising Secretary, 70, Brompton Road, London, S.W. 3.

Further copies of the Magazine may be had on application at a cost of 75p per season, or 15p individual copies.

'*Facts*'

Up-to-date looseleaf booklet on the activities of the A.E.W.L.A. 10p per copy, plus postage 5p, obtainable from Organising Secretary.

Kilt Pins, minature gilt Lacrosse kilt pins, 20p each, plus postage, obtainable from Organising Secretary.

Films

England v. U.S. Touring Team 1964

GBITT 1967 (Colour and Sound)

Enquiries to hire these films should be made to the Organising Secretary.

Lacrosse Loops

These may be obtained from:
Guy Butler, Harbledown, Little Hadham, Herts.